# JAPANESE COCKTAILS

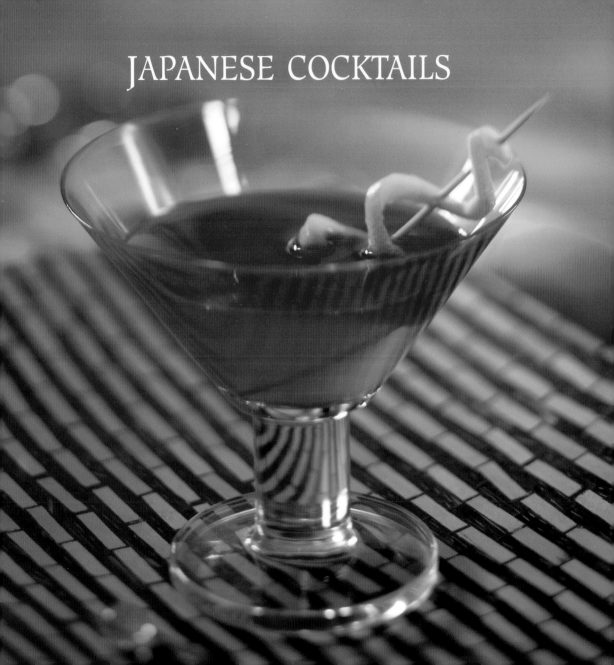

# JAPANESE COCKTAILS

## YURI KATO

CHRONICLE BOOKS
SAN FRANCISCO

Page 93 constitutes a continuation
of the copyright page.

ISBN: 978-0-8118-7511-0

Library of Congress Cataloging-in-
Publication Data available.

Manufactured in China.

Design by Elizabeth M. Watson.

This book has been set in
Hiroshige and Universe.

Hibiki 12 Year Old, Juhyo Special,
Kagura No Mai, Kakubin, Kuromaru,
Midori, Shirofuda, Torys Whisky,
Yaemaru, Yamazaki 12 Year Old,
Yamazaki 18 Year Old, and Zen Green
Tea Liqueur are trademarks of Suntory
International Corp.

10 9 8 7 6 5 4 3 2 1

Chronicle Books LLC
680 Second Street
San Francisco, California 94107

www.chroniclebooks.com

# Contents

# Introduction

Kagami Biraki is a traditional Japanese celebration usually observed at the start of a new year or on special occasions such as a company anniversary, wedding, or even the opening day of baseball season. The significance of this tradition is to wish for good fortune and good health. At the ceremony, the host breaks the top lid of a saké barrel, or *kagami,* with a wooden mallet, and the saké is shared with others.

For centuries, these types of ceremonies have included drinking as a big part of the Japanese culture. Saké is one of Japan's most distinctive alcoholic beverages, known to be shared among samurai warriors to keep them warm during winter battles. Shochu, another well-known Japanese drink, has been distilled in Japan for hundreds of years from a variety of ingredients, including rice, sweet potatoes, barley, and buckwheat. Japan also produces great whiskies and plum wines.

Today in Japan, you can buy a bottle of saké or whisky from vending machines on the street. My mother used to send my older sister and me to buy beer or saké from nearby vending machines for my father's dinner guests. Although the number of vending machines selling alcohol has decreased in an attempt to prevent underage drinking and drunk driving, you can still find them throughout Japan.

Drinking is an intrinsic part of traditional Japanese family culture. Many homes include a well-stocked liquor cabinet

◀ ◀ Zentini (see recipe on page 48)
◀ Saké *taru* for Kagami Biraki

7

▶ Suntory Kakubin whisky commercial

▼ Yakyu Kozo, or "Baseball Kid" panel, was created by Gekkeikan Saké in 1934 when major league baseball star Babe Ruth arrived in Japan.

To celebrate the arrival of the American home-run king, Baseball Kid signs were placed in front of liquor stores.

御家庭に
御来客に

with Japanese whisky, Scotch, bourbon, saké, and shochu. Sometimes you'll find a case of domestic beer, but alcohol like wine or *chu-hai*, canned cocktails, are not typically kept on hand. My father's generation of "salarymen," or businessmen, rarely drank wine and thought *chu-hai* cocktails were "for the younger drinkers."

Drinking and dining are an integral part of Japanese culture because they are shared together. It is not a Japanese custom to drink without eating, so there are not many bars that serve alcohol without food in Japan. Pairing food and cocktails may be new in some countries, but not in Japan.

While the legal drinking age in Japan is twenty, many younger than that experience the taste of alcohol at home with their parents at dinner (as in parts of Europe). For the younger generation, there is no sense of playing with fire when it comes to alcohol because it's introduced at a young age in the home.

I learned about drinking responsibly from my sister, who is six years older than I. She occasionally invited me to join her and her friends for a night out. There were times when she didn't drink at all despite her friends' offers. She usually did this when she knew she'd be driving. Back then, and

even in certain situations today, it was considered rude if you didn't accept a drink when it was offered. However, seeing my sister doing the right thing, I naturally understood that drinking and driving was not a cool thing to do.

In recent years, Japan has imposed new alcohol-related traffic laws. From 1996 to 2006, the number of alcohol-related accidents decreased by 47 percent as a result of stricter laws and lower blood alcohol content (BAC) caps. Today, Japan's legal blood alcohol limit is 0.03 grams (compared to 0.08 grams in the United States). Even cab companies require drivers to take breath tests before driving. Those tests can detect alcohol in the system from the day before, so it's best to assume that if you're suffering from a hangover, you should not be driving. In 2006 Japan's

Traffic Safety Administration began supporting the "handle keeper" campaign to promote driving with designated drivers.

In the past, many younger Japanese drinkers were not used to white spirits other than shochu, a distilled spirit made in Japan that's similar to vodka yet lighter in alcohol volume. Today, however, this is changing as more Japanese bartenders are learning about Western cocktail culture and mixing

▲ and ▶ Street vending machines selling beer and saké drinks
▶ ▶ Yamazaki Whisky Library from the Suntory Yamazaki Distillery
▼ Official "handle keeper" logo used by Japan's Traffic Safety Administration to encourage designated driving

cocktails with foreign spirits like rum, tequila, and gin.

My main educator, as with many young girls, was my mother. Although she didn't drink alcohol while I was growing up, she knew a lot about alcohol from stocking our home bar. She shopped at liquor stores every other week and bought saké, shochu, beer, and whiskies. I remember asking her about the difference between bourbon and Scotch, or sweet potato shochu and barley shochu, for example. She provided me with answers every time. It took me many years to learn about alcohol—and I am still learning. My mom was also a chef and shared her knowledge of food and alcohol pairing. For example, in the West, saké is often served with sushi, but in Japan, sushi can be paired with whisky or oolong *hai*

(shochu and oolong tea; see recipe on page 36).

Many of the cocktails featured in this book are served with fresh ingredients from the sea. Among my favorite ingredients are salmon eggs. When I go home to Japan, my brother-in-law's family from Hokkaido, the northern island of Japan, sends us fresh, local salmon eggs. I remember my mother marinating the eggs overnight in saké and soy sauce and serving them with shiso leaves over rice the next day. For generations, my family has learned never to compromise on ingredients, including those used in cocktails. Like good food, cocktails start with quality ingredients.

## Size Matters

The majority of cocktails in this book are fairly light in overall alcohol volume, compared to other concoctions on the market. In Japan, cocktails are not very strong. The base spirit, shochu, is only about 25 percent alcohol by volume compared to a regular bottle of vodka at 40 percent. In Japan, glassware is also a lot smaller than what's used in the United States. The bigger-the-better sensibility doesn't fit well in the Japanese cocktail culture, especially when drinking without eating. Cocktails are meant

▲ A traditional
*izakaya* bar sign
◀ A saké cup made
out of dried squid

to be enjoyed along with good company and good food.

## Ingredients

The majority of the ingredients used in the recipes in this book are available in the United States at gourmet food stores and international farmers' markets. You can also find items like yuzu juice, Calpis or Calpico, and Ramune soda on the Internet.

Try to use fresh fruits that are in season for the best taste. Fruits always remind me of a particular season; for example, watermelon means baseball season is here, and sweet potatoes signal the start of fall and cooler, shorter winter days ahead.

Also, look for specific varieties of fruits and vegetables, since the flavor varies from one region to another. For example, Fuji apples taste different from other types of apples, and tangerine oranges have sweeter juice than regular oranges. In fact, finding the right ingredients from gourmet stores and farmers' markets are an important part of mixology. Take your time in finding the right ingredients and enjoy the shopping experience. The reward will be in tasting the results.

My favorite Japanese fruit, *yuzu*, provides a distinctive flavor with a hint of

grapefruit and lemon. I also enjoy using *kabosu*, which gives a similar lime taste. It can make or break your drink because of its very strong flavor. When used properly, yuzu and *kabosu* can harmonize and enhance the other flavors in a cocktail in a fantastic way.

On the sweeter side, I decided to use gum syrup (often called sugar syrup) instead of simple syrup in this book because it is the standard syrup used in Japan. Gum syrup has a higher sugar content than regular simple syrup, which is usually a simple concoction of 50 percent sugar and 50 percent water. In gum syrup, gum arabic is added to water, and the sugar acts as an emulsifier to avoid sugar crystallizing, allowing water to be mixed with more sugar than in simple syrup. Some commercial gum syrups sold in Japan are mixed with other emulsifiers including gum. You can find gum syrup in gourmet food stores and on the Internet.

This book can also serve as a fun travel guide for learning more about Japan's history as well as our favorite spirits. If you have been to Japan before, you may recognize some of the local ingredients. If you've never visited, then use this book as a way to explore Japanese cocktails.

If you can't locate some ingredients, then maybe it's time to visit Japan. And take my advice, when you visit Japan for the first time, expect the unexpected—and be very thirsty. You can find more resources and photos online by visiting the Cocktail Times website at www.cocktailtimes.com. Let the journey begin. *Kanpai!*

# Saké cocktails

In Japan, the term *saké* refers to alcohol in general. Saké, as it's known in the West, is called *nihon-shu* in Japanese. There are about two thousand *nihon-shu* breweries, or *sakaguras*, making more than ten thousand brands of *nihon-shu*, according to the Japan Saké Brewers Association. Saké has been produced in Kyoto for centuries; for example, in the mid-1600s, there were more than eighty brewers in the Fushimi region of Kyoto alone.

*Nihon-shu* cannot really be described as a "rice wine" because technically it's not a wine or even a distilled spirit. *Nihon-shu* first goes through a similar production process to beer because it's made from grain ingredients. In the production of both *nihon-shu* and beer, brewers must first convert starch into sugar before adding yeast to convert sugar into alcohol, whereas wine makers already have the sugar present from the grapes. Unlike beer that contains 4 to 6 percent

alcohol, however, most *nihon-shu* is bottled at 14 to 16 percent alcohol, while wine is bottled at around 8 to 14 percent.

There are many different types and categories of *nihon-shu*. It is largely graded by the rice-polishing ratio on the label, which often determines the quality. For example, *ginjoshu* is a premium saké made from rice polished down to 60 percent or less. *Daiginjoshu* is a superpremium saké from rice polished down to 50 percent or

▼ In 1596, Toshimaya Juemon was the first to build a saké shop around Kanda-Kamakura riverbank, today known as the Kandabashi region. During the Edo period (1603-1868), Juemon was also known to be the first to brew *shirozaké*, a sweet white saké. *Shirozaké* is very similar to *amazaké*, though *shirozaké* contains a very small amount of alcohol. Traditionally, *shirozaké* is produced in late February in time for the Girls' Day Festival in March.

▲ This ball is called *sakabayashi* (or *sugitama*). *Saka* comes from the word "saké" and *bayashi* is synonymous with *hayashi*, which means "forest" in Japanese. It is made from layers of leaves and is usually placed in front of a *sakagura* (saké brewery) to announce that a new season of saké is being prepared. The ball is green in color, but the color will change as time passes, showing the aging or maturing of new saké.

less. *Nihon-shu* polished to at least 70 percent is called *honjoshu*. Futsushu means "normal saké," *namazaké* is not pastueurized, and *amazaké* is made from *saké kasu*, or saké lees, called *koji* (malted rice), and does not contain alcohol. *Nigori zaké* is unfiltered and usually sweeter than other sakés. The alcohol percentage, brewery name, production location, and the type of rice used to produce the saké can all be found on the bottle's label.

When purchasing a bottle of *nihon-shu*, enjoy it within a year from the date indicated on the label and store in a dark, cool place. Any direct light can damage *nihon-shu* and sometimes change its color. I remember my grandmother wrapping a bottle of *nihon-shu* with newspaper before storing it in order to avoid light exposure. Once a bottle of saké is opened, it's best to consume it within a day or two because once exposed to air, the taste begins to change. Store opened bottles in the refrigerator—especially *namazaké* because it's not pasteurized.

In Japan, *nihon-shu* is usually consumed straight and is rarely mixed in cocktails. I enjoy mixing cocktails with saké, and for a simple cocktail made with few ingredients, I usually use *daiginjo* saké in order to appreciate its quality.

# SAKÉ
## COCKTAIL RECIPES

*S
a
k
é

c
o
c
k
t
a
i
l
s*

The Japanese flag is often referred to as *hinomaru*. *Hi* means the sun and *maru* refers to the circle. Japan's national flag has a large red circle on a white background.

A simple bento box with one umeboshi on plain white rice is called *Hinomaru bento* because it looks like the Japanese flag.

## Hinomaru

**3 oz (90 ml) saké**

**Umeboshi (salty ume pickle)**

Heat saké by placing the *tokkuri* (saké flask) or an earthenware container in a bowl of hot water until warm (about 120° to 130°F or 50° to 55°C).

Place umeboshi in an *ochoko* cup and pour hot saké into the cup and serve.

20

## Bubble Shooter

1 tbsp salmon eggs
1 tbsp (15 ml)
   soy sauce
3 oz (90 ml)
   daiginjo saké
Gold flakes for
   garnish (optional)

Marinate salmon eggs in soy sauce overnight. Scoop them out of the soy sauce and place into a tall shot glass.

Pour saké over the eggs and garnish with gold flakes.

## Hotate-zaké

1 tsp butter
1 scallop, broiled
Fresh rosemary
1 oz (30 ml) daiginjo, hot

In a small saucepan over medium heat, add butter, scallop, and rosemary and heat for 1 to 2 minutes. Remove pan from the heat.

Pour hot saké over scallop and serve with chilled *daiginjo* saké.

## Butter of the Forest

¼ avocado, peeled and pitted
1 tsp (5 ml) honey
2 oz (60 ml) nigori zaké
½ oz (15 ml) citrus-flavored
    vodka
1 oz (30 ml) soymilk
Avocado slice for garnish

Muddle avocado with honey in a
mixing glass until smooth. Add
remaining ingredients and shake
with ice. Strain into a chilled
martini glass. Garnish with an
avocado slice and serve.

In Japan, avocado is referred to as *morino batah*, meaning "butter of the forest," because of its heavy, creamy texture.

# Zen Milk Bath

**1 oz (30 ml) Zen Green Tea Liqueur**
**1 oz (30 ml) nigori zaké**
**¹/₄ oz (7 ml) vanilla vodka**
**2 oz (60 ml) milk**
**Matcha powder for garnish**

Mix all ingredients in a cocktail shaker with ice. Strain into a chilled martini glass. Sprinkle matcha powder on top and serve.

# Saké Eggnog (Tamago Zaké)

**2 oz (60 ml) saké**
**1 raw egg**
**Sugar to taste (optional)**

Heat saké by placing a *tokkuri* (saké flask) or a small earthenware container in a hot bowl of water until warm (about 120° to 130°F or 50° to 55°C). Do not boil. Beat egg (with sugar, if preferred) with chopsticks in a small bowl. When saké is hot, pour into a Japanese tea cup and add the egg. Stir and serve.

Commonly known as *tamago zaké*, Saké Eggnog is a traditional cold remedy in Japan. (*Tamago* means "egg" in Japanese.) Even though it is an alcoholic beverage, it is consumed by both children and adults to combat colds in the way that chicken soup is consumed by Westerners.

## Momoha Bellini

$^1/_4$ **white peach**
$^1/_2$ **oz (15 ml)**
   **gum syrup**
**1 oz (30 ml)**
   **nigori zaké**
**3 oz (90 ml)**
   **sparkling wine**
   **or Champagne**

Muddle white peach with gum syrup in a mixing glass. Pour saké into peach-gum syrup and stir with ice to chill.

Strain mixture into a Champagne flute, top with sparkling wine, and serve.

## Samurai Courage

**3 oz (90 ml) daiginjo saké, hot**
**¹⁄₄ tsp yuzu juice**

Pour hot saké
and yuzu juice into
a saké *masu* (a
traditional Japanese
wooden saké cup)
and serve.

## Harajuku Fizz

2 oz (60 ml)
   nigori zaké
1 oz (30 ml) Calpis
   concentrate
1 oz (30 ml) freshly
   squeezed
   lemon juice
Ramune cider
Lemon wheel
   for garnish

Mix saké, Calpis, and lemon juice in a cocktail shaker with ice. Pour into a rocks glass and top with Ramune cider.

Garnish with lemon wheel and serve chilled.

Shibuya is one of the fashion districts in Tokyo. Among many clothing stores and restaurants, you'll find the most recognized building in Japan, Shibuya 109 (*ichi-maru-ku*) located just across from the Shibuya station. The building is packed with fashion-conscious young Japanese. From this district, you can make your way over to Harajuku, the district of J-pop. Crazed Japanese youngsters come here to enjoy all things pop, from J-pop music to idol posters. Girls dressed as anime heroines and characters often gather in this district. In the evening, head over to the Roppongi district. This is where you can find *gaijin*, or foreigners, as well as eateries from Irish and British pubs to American steakhouses. There are also a lot of fun bars and clubs in this district to explore.

## Shibuya 109

4 slices Japanese
   cucumber
6 fresh mint leaves
¼ oz (7 ml) umeshu
1 oz (30 ml) saké
1 oz (30 ml)
   apple juice
1 oz (30 ml)
   pineapple juice

Muddle cucumber and mint with *umeshu* in a mixing glass. Add saké, apple juice, pineapple juice, and ice and shake well.

Pour into a rocks glass and serve.

Saké cocktails

26

## Roppongi Hills

**4 fresh basil leaves**
**2 whole lychees**
**1 tsp (5 ml)**
  **gum syrup**
**3 oz (90 ml) saké**
**Club soda**

Muddle basil and
lychees with gum
syrup in a mixing
glass. Add saké
and stir.
   Pour into a
highball glass,
top with club soda,
and serve.

## CHERRY BLOSSOM SEASON

From March to April, cherry blossom viewing season, or Hanami, takes place all around Japan. In Okinawa, Japan's southern island, cherry blossoms can be seen as early as January. During these months, the people of Japan have *hanami* picnics under the trees. This season is also enjoyed with homemade bento and saké.

## Cherry Blossom (Sakura)

2 oz (60 ml) saké
1/2 tsp (2.5 ml) umeshu
1 tsp (2.5 ml) lemon juice
Sparkling wine
Maraschino cherry for garnish

Stir saké, *umeshu*, and lemon juice in a mixing glass with ice. Strain into a Champagne flute.

Top with sparkling wine, garnish with a maraschino cherry, and serve.

29

## Tsukiji Cup

**Saké**

**Shark fin, dried (*fuka hiré*)**

Heat saké by placing a *tokkuri* (saké flask) or an earthenware container in a hot bowl of water until warm (about 120° to 130°F or 50° to 55°C).

Pour while hot into an *ochoko* cup, drop a few dried shark fins on top, and serve.

## TOYKO TSUKIJI FISH MARKET

To find the most obscure ingredients in Japan, you'll need to wake up at 4 a.m. and head to Tokyo's Tsukiji Fish Market, where nearly three thousand tons of sea products are handled every day. This is also where the famous tuna auction takes place at 5 a.m. Dress accordingly—the fish market is full of busy vendors and wet concrete floors. You can explore everything from gigantic mussels and fatty tunas to squid saké cups and dried shark fins. Take Tokyo Metro Hibiya line to Tsukiji station to get to the market.

## OFFICE WORKERS

Professionals working in an office environment from 9 to 5 have nicknames—for a female it's OL, or "office lady," and for a male it's "salaryman."

## Office Lady

**6 fresh mint leaves**
**2 whole fresh straw-**
**berries, stemmed**
**and rinsed**
**1 tsp (5 ml) gum syrup**
**1 oz (30 ml) crème**
**de cassis**
**¹⁄₄ oz (7 ml)**
**lemon juice**
**¹⁄₂ oz (15 ml)**
**nigori zaké**
**Brut sparkling wine**

Muddle together mint and strawberries with gum syrup in a mixing glass. Add crème de cassis, lemon juice, saké, and ice and shake well. Strain into a martini glass. Discard the muddled strawberries and mint. Top with sparkling wine and serve.

# Salaryman

2 whole lychees
6 fresh mint leaves
   or lemongrass
$\frac{1}{2}$ tsp (2.5 ml)
   gum syrup
2 oz (60 ml) saké
2 oz (60 ml)
   grapefruit juice

Muddle lychees
and mint leaves
with gum syrup in
a mixing glass.
   Pour saké and
grapefruit juice over
the top of mixture
and serve.

# Shochu cocktails

Shochu is the oldest spirit made in Japan. It was produced as early as the fifteenth century. A spirit similar to shochu would be vodka, though shochu has a lot less alcohol content than vodka.

In the last several years, the image of shochu has drastically changed in the domestic market. Shochu used to be characterized as a drink enjoyed by middle-aged businessmen. Now, younger and older generations alike enjoy shochu in many ways, including on the rocks, with hot water, and in cocktails. Cocktails mixed with shochu are called *chu-hai*. When it's mixed with oolong tea, it's called oolong *hai*, and with lemon, it is lemon *hai*.

One reason why shochu is appealing to many health-conscious Japanese is because studies have shown that shochu may release more enzymes. This release helps with dissolving blood clots. Another reason for its popularity is that shochu has less alcohol content than a regular bottle of distilled spirits, translating to fewer calories.

In 1999, Japan created a new type of shochu sommelier program called "shochu advisor." According to the Food & Beverage Specialists Organization, there are currently about ten thousand shochu advisors in Japan with professional knowledge of shochu and other types of alcohol,

▼ Shochu varieties, from left: *imo jochu* (sweet potato shochu), *kome jochu* (rice shochu), and *mugi jochu* (barley shochu)

including foreign spirits. A certified shochu advisor is also well versed in food and glassware, knowledge that enhances the experience of shochu. Anyone can apply for the license, but many shochu advisors are employed in the hospitality industry.

Shochu is made from a variety of ingredients, including *kome* (rice), *satsumaimo* (sweet potato), *mugi* (barley), and *soba* (Japanese buckwheat). Today, shochus are also made from nonconventional ingredients like chestnut, milk, and shiso leaves. There are more than six hundred shochu makers in Japan. While saké is produced all around Japan, Japan's southernmost island, Kyushu, is unsuitable for brewing saké because *moromi*, or the main mash used for saké

fermentation, goes bad quickly in Kyushu's warmer climates. This region has instead become famous for its shochus, which can be distilled in warmer temperatures.

The Kagoshima prefecture in Kyushu produces more shochus than any other part of Japan, with nearly one hundred shochu makers. Historically, the signature ingredient in Kagoshima shochu is sweet potato. Shochu made from sweet potato is called *imo jochu*. Sweet potato, or *satsumaimo*, shochus have a distinctive, freshly steamed potato aroma and full-bodied flavor. A small number of shochu distillers also use sugarcane as a base ingredient. Traditionally, in the Kagoshima prefecture, shochu is served with hot water in *roku-yon* style; *roku* means "six" and *yon* "four." Six parts shochu is mixed with four parts hot water to decrease the alcohol content to around 15 percent, about the same amount as saké.

*Imo jochu* has an intense and distinctive aroma compared to *mugi jochu* (barley shochu) or *kome jochu* (rice shochu). When I use *imo jochu* in

▶ From left: Kagura No Mai is distilled from buckwheat in Miyazaki prefecture. Kuromaru and Yaemaru are both produced in Kagoshima prefecture, which is famous for its sweet potato shochus. Juhyo Special is made from a mixture of corn, barley, and rice—ideal for mixing *chuhai* cocktails.

cocktails, I am particularly careful with the amount of *imo jochu* added, because if too much is used, the intense flavor of *imo jochu* can overpower the other ingredients.

Shochu distillers must first make *koji*, propagated rice or barley. *Koji* changes the starch of the ingredients, whether it's sweet potato or rice, into glucose. In the first fermentation, yeast is added to turn the rice or barley glucose into alcohol. In the second fermentation, the steamed ingredients are mixed in. Then, the fermented mash, or *moromi*, is distilled. Up until the distillation process, the making of shochu is very similar to saké. Shochu production first began from using saké's *moromi* hundreds of years ago.

There are two types of shochus: *korui* shochu and *honkaku* shochu, also known as *otsurui* shochu. *Korui* shochu is distilled several times to produce pure alcohol. This type of shochu is similar to vodka because they both provide a tasteless and odorless spirit base. However, *honkaku* shochu provides full flavors and aromas. Each *honkaku* shochu brand comes with distinct flavor profiles and aromas based on its ingredients and local distillation culture.

The Okinawa prefecture produces its own distinct style of shochu called *awamori*. While most shochus are bottled with about 25 percent alcohol, *awamori* is bottled with 30 percent. It is made from Thai rice (*indica*), thus the flavor is quite different from other *kome jochu*. Production of *awamori* began as early as the fifteenth century during the Ryukyu dynasty. At that time, the Ryukyu Islands traded with China and countries in Southeast Asia, importing a variety of goods that included distilled spirits from Thailand (then called Siam). Thai distillation was soon introduced to Okinawa, and the locals began producing a spirit named *awamori*. The dynasty operated its distillery near Shuri Castle and produced *awamori* for the Shogunate government of Edo and China.

▼ *Chu-hai* cocktail products from left: Ginza Cocktail Melon, Mugi Honkaku Mizuwari (barley shochu with water), Oolong Hai (oolong tea and shochu), Sorekara (*imo jochu* with water)

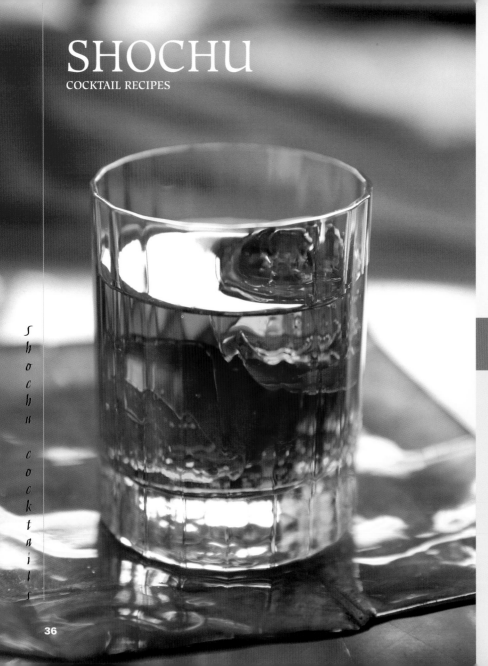

# SHOCHU
## COCKTAIL RECIPES

## Oolong Hai

2 oz (60 ml) Yaemaru
mugi jochu (barley
shochu)
4 oz (120 ml)
oolong tea

Pour both ingredients
into an old-fashioned
glass over three large
ice cubes and serve
chilled.

### OOLONG HAI

Oolong Hai is served
at most *izakaya* bars
that offer a variety of
small dishes, including
traditional Japanese
dishes like sashimi,
tempura, and vegetable
dishes. Oolong Hai
goes well with all
types of dishes,
whether they're raw
or deep-fried.

# Yuzu Bath

2¹/₂ oz (75 ml)
   Yaemaru
   mugi jochu
   (barley shochu)
¹/₄ oz (7 ml)
   yuzu juice
¹/₄ oz (7 ml)
   Triple Sec
Lemon peel for
   garnish

Mix all ingredients
except the lemon
peel in a cocktail
shaker with ice.
   Strain into a
chilled martini glass
and garnish with
lemon peel.

# Hot Yuzu Bath

2 oz (60 ml) Juhyo Special shochu, hot
¹/₄ oz (7 ml) yuzu juice
1 tsp (5 ml) honey

Pour all ingredients into an
*ochoko* cup and serve hot.

## YUZU BATH

Yuzu is a Japanese citrus fruit that tastes
like grapefruit with a hint of lemon. In the
winter months, Japanese people often drop a
few yuzu into a hot bath because the fruit is
known to warm up the body. There are a
number of beauty products in Japan that
contain yuzu. Saké is also known to be good
for the skin because it contains amino acids
and peptides, which improve skin tone.

# Bloody Mari-Chan

2 oz (60 ml) Juhyo
   Special shochu
4 oz (120 ml) tomato
   juice
¼ tsp tonkatsu
   sauce
¼ tsp lemon juice
Pinch shichimi
   togarashi spice
Stick Japanese
   cucumber for
   garnish
Shiso leaf for garnish

Mix all ingredients
except garnishes
in a cocktail shaker
with ice.
    Pour into a
highball glass.
Garnish with a
cucumber stick and
fresh shiso leaf
and serve.

Shochu cocktails

## SHICHIMI TOGARASHI SPICE

Kyoto is famous for its *shichimi togarashi* spice. This mixed spice contains seven different seasonings: *togarashi* or red chili, *sansho* or Szechuan pepper, sesame seeds, seaweed, dried mandarin orange peel, black hemp seeds, and white poppy seeds.

# Tokyo Dome

**2 oz (60 ml) Yaemaru mugi jochu
(barley shochu)**
**3¹/₂ (105 ml) oz apple juice**
**1 tsp (5 ml) freshly squeezed lemon juice**
**Ginger ale**
**Orange spiral for garnish**

Mix shochu, apple juice, and lemon juice
in a cocktail shaker with ice.

Pour into a short glass and top
with ginger ale.

Garnish with an orange
spiral and serve.

# Koshien Cooler

**1 oz (30 ml) Midori
melon liqueur**
**¹/₂ oz (15 ml)
Juhyo Special
shochu**
**1 ¹/₂ oz (45 ml)
pineapple juice**
**¹/₄ oz (7 ml) fresh
lemon juice**
**3 oz (90 ml) club
soda**

Mix Midori, shochu,
pineapple juice, and
lemon juice in a
cocktail shaker with
ice. Strain into a
highball glass over
fresh ice, top with
club soda, and
serve.

Tokyo Dome is the home of the Tokyo Yomiuri Giants baseball team. The Giants are the most popular baseball team in Japan, similar to the New York Yankees in America. Like the Yankees, the Giants have their own rival, the Osaka Hanshin Tigers. Rivalry between the Giants and the Tigers is very much like the relationship between the Yankees and the Red Sox in the American League.

There is also a cultural rivalry between the Kanto and Kansai regions. Kanto is the area that includes Tokyo, Yokohama, and the surrounding areas, while Kansai includes Osaka, Nara, Kyoto, and nearby regions. It is akin to the rivalry between the East Coast and the West Coast in the United States. There are Central and Pacific leagues in Japan—and the Giants and Tigers are in the Central League.

If you have a chance to watch a game at either Koshien, the home field of the Tigers, or the Tokyo Dome, watch the fans—they may offer more entertainment than the game itself. When the Tigers win at home, the fans stay in the stadium after the game and sing theme songs to celebrate. When the stadium shuts down, the fans find their way to local bars near the stadium and continue celebrating.

Visit the official website of the Tokyo Dome for directions and other information at www.tokyo-dome.co.jp/e and visit www.hanshin.co.jp/koshien for Koshien. (Tip: The Koshien stadium opens two to three hours prior to the game. There is no stadium parking, and they do not allow parking on most streets around the stadium, so you'll want to take the Hanshin train. There are several trains available to the Tokyo Dome.)

▲ Osaka Hanshin Tigers' mascot enjoying saké, or *nihon-shu*

## Enoshima Swizzle

¹/₂ green kiwi,
cut into chunks
¹/₂ tsp (2.5 ml)
gum syrup
2 oz (60 ml)
Yaemaru
mugi jochu
(barley shochu)
¹/₄ tsp yuzu juice
Club soda
Lime wedge
for garnish

Muddle kiwi with
gum syrup in a
cocktail shaker. Add
shochu and juice
and shake with ice.
Pour into a Collins
glass and top with
club soda.
Garnish with
a lime wedge
and serve.

### ENOSHIMA

Enoshima is a
beach town and
vacation getaway
in the Kanagawa
prefecture. The best
time to visit is July
through August to
see the fireworks
near the beach. The
town also has great
casual restaurants.
The restaurants on
the beach are called
beach houses. To get
to the beach, take
the Odakyu line from
the Shinjuku train
station in Tokyo to
the Fujisawa station.
For more infor-
mation about
Enoshima Beach,
go to the official
website at www.
cityfujisawa.ne.jp/
kankou/english/
point/beach.html.

Shochu cocktails

# Karuizawa Martini

4 fresh
raspberries,
rinsed
2 whole lychees
¼ oz (7 ml)
umeshu
2½ oz (75 ml)
Juhyo Special
shochu
Fresh rosemary
sprig for garnish

Muddle raspberries,
lychees, and *umeshu*
in a mixing glass.
  Add shochu and
mix with ice. Strain
the mixture through
a tea strainer into a
chilled martini glass.
  Garnish with
rosemary sprig
and serve.

Karuizawa is a
resort town in the
Nagano prefecture.
The town is a
popular vacation
destination for those
living in Tokyo and
the surrounding
areas because it's
a quick getaway
spot from the city.
Karuizawa hosted
events in the Summer
Olympics in 1964 as
well as the Winter
Olympics in 1996.
It is the only city
in the world that
has hosted both
summer and winter
Olympic events.

## Okinawa Nectar

2 oz (60 ml) awamori

2 oz (60 ml) peach nectar

$1/2$ oz (15 ml) pear-flavored vodka

$1/2$ oz (15 ml) rosemary-infused syrup

$1/4$ oz (7 ml) kabosu juice

Fresh rosemary sprig for garnish

Mix all ingredients except rosemary in a cocktail shaker with ice.

Strain into a chilled martini glass, garnish with a rosemary sprig, and serve.

# Kyusu Sour

2 oz (60 ml)
  Kuromaru imo
  jochu (sweet
  potato shochu)
1 oz (30 ml)
  pineapple juice
1 oz (30 ml) aloe
  vera juice
4 oz (120 ml)
  club soda
Pineapple wedge
  for garnish

Mix shochu,
pineapple juice,
and aloe vera
juice in a cocktail
shaker with ice.
  Strain into a
highball glass over
fresh ice and top
with club soda.
  Garnish with a
pineapple wedge
and serve.

Sour drinks are a
popular refreshment
in Japan. They
are available at
most *izakaya* bars
and other chain
restaurants serving
alcoholic beverages.
They are commonly
made by mixing
shochu and freshly
squeezed fruit juice
and topping with
soda. Sometimes
the menu may
read *nama shibori*,
meaning that the
fruit juice is freshly
squeezed.

## Love Hotel

1¹/₂ oz (45 ml) Juhyo Special shochu
2¹/₂ oz (75 ml) pink grapefruit juice
1¹/₂ oz (45 ml) rosé wine
**Lemon peel for garnish**

Mix shochu and grapefruit juice in a cocktail shaker with ice. Strain mixture into a chilled martini glass.

Top with rosé wine, garnish with a lemon peel, and serve.

## LOVE HOTELS

In Japan, many young adults live with their parents, so "love hotels" are places where couples can be together. Most love hotels offer *kyukei*, or rest packages (i.e., places to go for a couple of hours), or overnight accommodations. Hours and rates vary and most of these types of hotels do not take reservations.

## Meditation

2 oz (60 ml) kome jochu (rice shochu)
3 oz (90 ml) hoji tea, hot
1 oz (30 ml) freshly squeezed lemon juice
**Lemon zest**
**Lemon wedge for garnish (optional)**

Pour shochu, tea, and lemon juice into an *ocha* tea cup. Sprinkle lemon zest on top and place a lemon wedge on the side, if desired.

For variation, replace lemons with Meyer lemons.

## Monbulan (Mont Blanc)

1 oz (30 ml) Kuromaru imo jochu (sweet
   potato shochu)
1 oz (30 ml) cognac
1 $\frac{1}{2}$ oz (45 ml) chestnut purée
   with vanilla cloves
$\frac{1}{2}$ oz (15 ml) white chocolate liqueur
1 oz (30 ml) half-and-half
Chestnut chunks for garnish

Mix all ingredients except chestnut in
a cocktail shaker with ice. Strain into a
chilled martini glass.

    Garnish with chestnut chunks and serve.

## MONBULAN CAKE

*Monbulan* is a Japanese chestnut cake
named after the shape of Mont Blanc, in
the European Alps located between France
and Italy. *Monbulan* can be found in most
gourmet sections of food stores
in Japan.

Zen gardens, or Japanese rock gardens, are composed of sand, rocks, and grass, as well as other natural elements, in a minimalist style. One of the most famous Zen gardens can be seen at Ryoanji Temple, located northwest of Kyoto. The Ryoanji Temple's Zen garden is known for its *karasansui* style, which emphasizes rocks and sand rather than plants and flowers. The Ryoanji Temple is recognized as a historic monument in ancient Kyoto.

Originally, the Fujiwara family's estate garden was said to have been built in the late 1400s during the Muromachi period (1392–1573). It is still not known for certain today who designed the garden originally. To find out more about the Ryoanji Temple, visit the website www.ryoanji.jp.

▶ Zen Green Tea Liqueur

## Zentini

$^1/_2$ oz (15 ml) Zen
   Green Tea Liqueur
2 oz (60 ml) Juhyo
   Special shochu
Lemon peel for
   garnish

Stir the liqueur and shochu in a mixing glass with ice. Strain into a chilled martini glass, garnish with a lemon peel, and serve.

*Shochu cocktails*

48

# Salty Hachiko Dog

**2 oz (60 ml) Juhyo Special shochu**
**3 oz (90 ml) grapefruit juice**
**½ tsp (2.5 ml) lemon juice**
**Salt for glass rimming**

Mix shochu and grapefruit juice in a cocktail shaker with ice. Coat the rim of the cocktail glass with lemon and dip into salt.

Strain mixture into the rimmed cocktail glass and serve.

## MEET ME AT HACHIKO

In 1923, an akita dog named Hachiko was born and adopted by Eizaburo Uenoa, a university professor in Tokyo. Each morning Hachiko walked with Dr. Ueno to Shibuya station to see him off to work.

At the end of the workday, Hachiko would again return to the station to meet the professor. In 1925, the professor passed away from a stroke at the university and never came home. Hachiko, however, continued waiting for Dr. Ueno until Hachiko died in 1934. The Shibuya station is one of the most famous meeting spots in Japan.

## Hokkaido Martini

1 oz (30 ml)
   **Kuromaru imo
   jochu (sweet
   potato shochu)**
1 oz (30 ml)
   **vanilla cognac**
¹⁄₂ (15 ml) oz
   **half-and-half**
¹⁄₄ oz (7 ml) white
   **crème de cacao**
¹⁄₄ oz (7 ml)
   **sugarcane juice**
**Freshly ground
   nutmeg for
   garnish**

Mix all ingredients
except nutmeg in
a cocktail shaker
with ice.
   Strain into a
martini glass,
garnish with
ground nutmeg,
and serve.

## SAPPORO SNOW FESTIVAL

During a week in February, the famous Snow Festival (Yuri Matsuri) takes place in Sapporo, Hokkaido. It is one of the largest winter events in Japan, attracting nearly two million visitors every year. The festival began in 1950, when local high school students built six snow statues in Odori Park, located in downtown Sapporo. Today, the park is center stage for the Sapporo Snow Festival. An area in the park covering about twelve blocks is transformed into a snow museum, displaying snow and ice sculptures. To find out more about the Sapporo Snow Festival, visit www.snowfes.com/english/index.html.

## Sea of Japan

**1 oz (30 ml) kome**
**jochu (rice shochu)**
**1 tsp (5 ml) kabosu**
**juice**
**1 oz (30 ml)**
**tomato juice**
**1 tsp (5 ml) neriume**
**(salty plum paste)**
**1 oyster**

Mix all ingredients
except oyster in
a cocktail shaker
with ice.

Strain into a tall
shot glass over an
oyster and ice and
serve chilled.

You can also try
substituting *neriume*
with umeboshi.
Remove the pit
from the umeboshi
and muddle.

## Shiso Ume Mojito

**1 green shiso leaf**
**4 lime chunks**
**¹/₂ red umeboshi**
**(salty ume pickle)**
**¹/₂ tsp (2.5 ml)**
**gum syrup**
**2 oz (60 ml) Yaemaru**
**mugi jochu**
**(barley shochu)**
**or awamori**
**Club soda**
**Lime wedge for**
**garnish**

Cut shiso leaf
into small pieces.
Muddle shiso, lime,
umeboshi, and gum
syrup in a mixing
glass. Add shochu
and ice.

Shake and pour
into a short glass and
top off with club soda.

Garnish with a lime
wedge and serve.

## Yokohama Breeze

2 oz (60 ml)
  Yaemaru mugi
  jochu
  (barley shochu)
2 oz (60 ml)
  grapefruit juice
1 oz (30 ml) white
  cranberry juice
Sparking wine
Grapefruit peel for
  garnish

Mix shochu,
grapefruit juice,
and cranberry juice
in a cocktail shaker
with ice.

Strain into a
Champagne flute
and top with
sparkling wine.

Garnish with
a grapefruit peel
and serve.

Yokohama is the second largest city in Japan after Tokyo.
When the city first opened its port in 1859, the population was
just under 600. Today this major port city boasts a population
of about 3.5 million. There are many sightseeing areas in
Yokohama, including Minato Mirai 21 (MM21), Chinatown,
and the Motomachi area, among a few.

At MM21 you'll find the Yokohama Landmark Tower, which
is the tallest building in Japan, along with a large Ferris wheel
called the Cosmo Clock 21. The MM21 project was managed
by the City of Yokohama and designed in a futuristic style. The
name was chosen by the people of Yokohama in 1981. (*Minato*
means "port" and *Mirai* refers to "future.") To find out more
about Yokohama, visit www.city.yokohama.jp/ert.

◀ Yokohama Port

## Hanabi

1 1/2 oz (45 ml)
  wasabi shochu
2 1/2 oz (75 ml)
  tomato juice
1/4 oz (7 ml)
  lemon juice
1 tsp (5 ml) tonkatsu
  sauce
Dried red pepper
  for garnish

Mix all ingredients
except red pepper in
a cocktail shaker
with ice.

Pour mixture into
a tall glass, garnish
with a dried red
pepper, and serve.

*Hanabi* is a
Japanese term for
"fireworks."

# Whisky cocktails

Japan is recognized as one of the "big five" whisky-producing countries, along with Ireland, Scotland, Canada, and the United States. The origin of Japanese whisky is traced to its spelling, almost always written without an "e," like Scotch whisky, because the Japanese learned to distill whisky from the Scots in the early 1900s. Japanese whiskies may be smoky compared to bourbon or Canadian whiskies, but the majority of Japanese whiskies have a lighter flavor when compared to Scotch.

The most well-known whisky distiller in Japan is Suntory, which controls nearly 60 percent of the nation's whisky market. To learn more about its whisky, visit Suntory's signature Yamazaki Distillery located between Osaka and Kyoto stations. The distillery provides production tours and tasting seminars, as well as a variety of historic displays. The company imports more than seventy brands of distilled spirits and liqueurs and nearly 1,500 wines from more than twenty countries worldwide.

▲ Hibiki 12 Year Old, blended with more than 30 handcrafted, specially aged whiskies

◀ A building in Osaka features the high-end Japanese whisky, Hibiki, from Suntory

▶ Whisky stills
at the Yamazaki
Distillery

▼ The Yamazaki
single-malt whisky
18 years old

▼ Torys Whisky
Black and ▶ its
advertising
campaign

Suntory also produces and markets other types of beverages, including brandy, wine, shochu, soft drinks, water, and tea.

The first Suntory Old whisky was developed in November 1940, although World War II interrupted production, so it was not available until 1950. From 1950 to 1960, Suntory Old became popular among Japanese "salarymen" as a symbolic drink for older men. By 1970, more than a hundred thousand cases of Suntory Old were sold in domestic markets, and by the 1980s, the brand had sold more than a million cases. In the 1980s and 1990s, during the height of the booming Japanese

◁ ◁ The Suntory
Old Whisky
◁ Suntory Shirofuda
Whisky from 1932

▲ and ▶ The late
Shirijiro Torii, founder
of Suntory

▼ Suntory
Old"Mizuwari"
canned cocktails

*Whisky cocktails*

◄ Yamazaki
Distillery displays

economy, whisky became a drink of status. Among all the imported whiskies and brandies coming into the Japanese market, Suntory Old remains popular among middle-aged Japanese men as a reliable, familiar blended whisky.

# WHISKY
## COCKTAIL RECIPES

## Black Ship

1 $\frac{1}{2}$ oz (45 ml)
   Hibiki 12 Year Old
1 oz (30 ml)
   pomegranate
   juice
$\frac{1}{4}$ oz (7 ml) port
1 tsp (5 ml) lemon
   juice
Lemon peel
   for garnish

Mix all ingredients
except lemon peel
in a cocktail shaker
with ice.

   Strain into a
chilled martini glass,
garnish with lemon
peel, and serve.

## MATTHEW C. PERRY

In 1853, Matthew C. Perry, an American commodore, arrived in Japan to try to end Japan's 250-year-long isolationist era, or *heikoku*. During this period, many countries tried to open up relations with Japan, but none succeeded, until Perry arrived. On his arrival, he came with gifts from the West, including telescopes, maps, perfume, and whiskies. Perhaps it was Perry who taught the Japanese how to conduct business over a glass of whisky.

Today, hundreds of Japanese raise their glasses and toast to the arrival of Perry and the end of the period of isolation. Each May at the Shimoda Port in the Shizuoka prefecture, Kurofune Matsuri, meaning "black ship festival," after Perry's black ship, is held to celebrate his arrival with fireworks, a parade, marine exhibitions, and more. Visit the City of Shimoda's website at www.shimoda-city.info/index_e.html for more information.

# Mizuwari

Mizuwari is perhaps the most well-known drink in Japan. *Mizu* means "water" and *wari* means "to cut." Diluting or cutting whisky with ice and water is the most common way to drink whisky in Japan. To order mizuwari, raise your hand and say, "*mizuwari kudasai*!" ("mizuwari please!"). A good mizuwari appears easy to make, but according to many professional Japanese bartenders, the perfect mizuwari takes care and attention.

The art of making a perfect mizuwari is similar to making a martini. Like a martini, a mizuwari can be made many different ways. The amount of water and whisky is important, as well as the size and amount of ice you add. One company believes in the "mizuwari 1-2-3" method: one part whisky, two parts mineral water, and three large ice cubes.

Here is how I make my mizuwari: First, place two large ice cubes made with mineral water in a glass. Then pour one part of your favorite Japanese whisky and one part mineral water. The ice cubes will keep the temperature at around 60°F (15°C) for one hour or long enough to finish the drink.

Some bars in Japan make their own mizuwari ice by shaving the ice to form the perfect round figure. The stirring is also important, according to Suntory. The company developed their own formula called "thirteen times and one-half" — stirring thirteen and one-half times to create the perfect drink.

# Gion

1 oz (30 ml)
   Hibiki
   12 Year Old
¼ oz (7 ml)
   Campari
2 oz (60 ml)
   pomegranate
   juice
¼ oz (7 ml)
   crème de cassis
¼ oz (7 ml)
   freshly squeezed
   lemon juice
Hajikami (ginger
   pickled in
   sweet vinegar)
   for garnish

Shake all
ingredients except
*hajikami* in a
cocktail shaker
with ice.
   Strain into a
chilled martini
glass, garnish
with *hajikami*,
and serve.

## GION FESTIVAL

A visit to Gion in Kyoto is a must for those interested in history. Most of the architecture in the Gion district is very traditional. Many Japanese and foreign visitors come to this area to see geisha girls, or *geiko*. However, the streets are kept very quiet out of respect for this historic area.

Throughout July, one of the largest festivals of the year, the Gion Festival (Gion Matsuri) is celebrated with parades, food and drink, and live *taiko* drum performances. The Yasaka shrine (which used to be named Gion) is the center stage of the festival. The origin of Gion Matsuri goes back to 869, when a plague spread throughout Kyoto and other parts of the country. Locals began to pray to the Gion God at the temple and soon the disease disappeared. To find out more about Gion Matsuri visit the website at www.gionmatsuri.jp/.

# Oyaji

**1 orange slice**
**2 maraschino**
   **cherries**
**¹/₂ tsp (2.5 ml)**
   **gum syrup**
**2 oz (60 ml)**
   **Yamazaki**
   **12 Year Old**
**Club soda**

Muddle the orange slice, maraschino cherries, and gum syrup in an old-fashioned glass. Fill the glass with ice cubes.

Pour whisky into the glass, top with club soda, and serve.

*Oyaji* is Japanese jargon for a middle-aged man. The drink is a Japanese version of an old-fashioned cocktail.

# Maneki-Tini

1 ½ oz (45 ml)
   Hibiki
   12 Year Old
1 tsp sweet
   vermouth
¼ oz (7 ml)
   cherry brandy
Maraschino cherry
   for garnish

Mix all ingredients
except cherry in a
cocktail shaker
with ice.
   Strain into a
chilled martini
glass.
   Garnish with
a maraschino
cherry and serve.

Maneki Neko statues are often seen at Japanese restaurants and bars. They are known as fortune cats or lucky cats and are thought to bring good luck to the owner of a business. *Maneki* means "welcome," and *neko* means "cat."

## Tokyo Sidecar

2 oz (60 ml)
  Yamazaki
  12 Year Old
1 oz (30 ml)
  Triple Sec
$1/4$ tsp yuzu juice

Mix all ingredients in a cocktail shaker with ice.
  Strain into a chilled martini glass and serve.

## Torys High

**3 parts Torys whisky**

**7 parts Suntory Premium Soda**

**¹/₂ lemon wheel for garnish**

First add Torys whisky, then ice cubes,
to a tall glass.

Pour soda on top and stir.

Garnish with a lemon wheel and serve.

## UNCLE TORYS

Suntory introduced Torys whisky in 1919, named after the company's founder, Shinjiro Torii. It was an immediate success. In 1958, a new Torys whisky character, Uncle Torys, was born. The character was shy around women and sensitive to his family and friends. His personality helped the brand to connect with its target consumers throughout the years.

As Torys whisky grew in popularity, the company established a chain of bars called Torys Bars across the country. The bars served its signature cocktail, Torys High, a simple concoction of Torys whisky and club soda with a lemon garnish. Most were neighborhood bars where Japanese salarymen stopped after work. Today, some of the Torys Bars are still open, though they're not as popular.

To taste a real Torys High, visit one of the oldest Torys Bars in Juso, Osaka, located just outside Juso station (Hankyu-Kobe line). Mr. Eiji Egawa is a second-generation owner and has worked there for 30 years. Try Egawa's signature drink, Blueberry Hill, the winning cocktail of the 1987 Suntory Cocktail Competition. It's a simple concoction mixed with Jack Daniel's Tennessee Whiskey, crème de myrtille (blueberry flavor), and lemon juice. The drink is served straight up in a martini glass.

## Yuzu Julep

**6 fresh mint leaves**
**1 tsp (5 ml)**
**gum syrup**
**2 oz (60 ml)**
**Yamazaki**
**12 Year Old**
**$^{1}/_{2}$ oz (15 ml)**
**yuzu juice**
**Fresh mint sprig**
**for garnish**

Muddle mint leaves with gum syrup in a mixing glass. Pour into a short glass with crushed ice.

Add whisky and yuzu juice, garnish with a mint sprig, and serve.

## Echo Julep

**6 fresh mint leaves**
**1 tsp (5 ml) gum**
**syrup**
**Crushed Ice**
**2 oz (60 ml) Hibiki**
**12 Year Old**
**$^{1}/_{2}$ oz (15 ml) yuzu**
**juice**
**Fresh mint sprig for**
**garnish**

Muddle mint leaves with gum syrup in a silver julep cup. Fill cup with crushed ice, add whisky and yuzu juice, and stir.

Garnish with a mint sprig and serve.

*Hibiki* refers to "echoes" in Japanese.

# More cocktails

In earlier chapters, you'll find cocktail recipes prepared with Japan's distinctive beverages like saké, shochu, and Japanese whisky. This chapter takes you beyond the more well-known, Japanese-inspired cocktails and infuses recipes with other types of spirits, including vodka, rum, and tequila, to name a few. Except for two traditional recipes made with *umeshu* and Denki Bran, the other cocktails in this chapter are original. Many of the recipes have taken on a fun, modern-classic twist, such as the Kabosu Gimlet and Yuzu Mojito, which are both among my favorites!

If you're looking for a popular Japanese-infused cocktail, try the Homemade Umeshu. This recipe is from my mother, who makes her own every other year. I remember helping her prepare this drink by making small holes in plums before adding them to the jar so that the flavor of the plums would be released during the infusion process. In the first few years, we would watch as the color grew darker, finally

reaching its medium amber color, as shown on page 72. When ready to serve, try the *umeshu* straight with or without ice, or mixed with soda. Or, for a great-tasting variation, mix it with Champagne.

▼ Suntory Home Cocktail Competition ad (1956)

# MORE
## COCKTAIL RECIPES

### Homemade Umeshu

RECIPE BY KIYOMI KATO

**20–25 fresh green ume**

**1 cup (250 ml)**
  **rock sugar**

**1.8 quarts (1.7 liters)**
  **white liquor**
  **or vodka**

Clean the glass infusion jar and fresh green ume and dry thoroughly. Poke several holes in each ume with a toothpick. Place ume, then rock sugar on top into jar. If you can't find rock sugar, substitute with 1 cup (250 ml) honey or white sugar. Pour white liquor over.

Place the jar in a dark, cool area, away from direct light. Infusion takes about six months to a year. After one year, take out the ume and transfer the liquid into a different glass container.

# Ajisai

1 oz (30 ml) blanco tequila
1 oz (30 ml) namazaké
1/2 oz (15 ml) blue curaçao
2 oz (60 ml) pineapple juice
1/4 oz (7 ml) lime juice

1/2 oz (15 ml) agave nectar
Akajiso salt (red shisho) for garnish (see Note)

Mix all ingredients
except salt in a
cocktail shaker
with ice.

Pour into a rocks
glass rimmed with
*akajiso* salt.

Decorate the
drink with a cocktail
umbrella and serve.

*Note: To make
akajiso salt, grind
red shiso. Mix 2 parts
red shiso with 1 part
salt and 1/4 part
sugar.*

June is the month of
the Japanese rainy
season, or *tsuyu doki*.
The *ajisai* (hydrangea)
flower blooms during
this time. The historic
regions of Kamakura
and Hakone are
famous for their *ajisai*
flowers. They are most
commonly blue, but
you can also find
them in pink, purple,
and white.

73

## Aloe Margarita

1 1/2 oz (45 ml)
   blanco tequila
3 oz (90 ml) aloe
   vera juice
Juice of 1/2 lime
1 tsp (5 ml) lemon
   juice
Salt for glass rim
Lime wedge
   for garnish

Mix all liquid
ingredients in a
cocktail shaker
with ice.
   Pour into a salt-
rimmed glass and
garnish with a
lime wedge.

## Chaniwa

1 oz (30 ml) Zen
   Green Tea liqueur
1/4 oz (7 ml) banana
   liqueur
1 oz (30 ml) light
   rum
2 scoops vanilla
   ice cream
2 biscuits
Banana slices
   for garnish
Matcha powder
   for garnish

Mix green tea
liqueur, banana
liqueur, rum, and ice
cream in a blender
until smooth. Break
biscuits into pieces,
add, and stir.
   Pour into a chilled
martini glass. Place
a few banana slices
on top and sprinkle
with matcha powder.
Serve with a spoon.

## CHANIWA

*Chaniwa* is part of a Zen garden that connects the outside garden with stepping stones that lead to a main tearoom, or *cha shitsu*. Literally, *cha* means "tea" and *niwa* refers to a garden. Along the stepping stone path, a stone water basin, or *tsukabai*, is often placed for guests to wash their hands before entering the room. *Chaniwa* areas are not always open to the public.

### Denki Bran

**2 oz (60 ml) Denki Bran**

Serve straight up at room temperature.

## THE OLDEST COCKTAIL IN JAPAN?

The Kamiya Bar opened in 1880 in Asakusa, Tokyo, and claims to be the first bar to be established in Japan. Its signature cocktail, Denki Bran, is sold in a bottle at the counter window and in the restaurant. Denki Bran is a brandy-based liqueur cocktail bottled at 30 percent alcohol. It is blended with gin, wine, and various herbs. During the Meiji era (1868–1912), electricity was still rare, thus many products were named *denki* ("electric") to signal something new. *Bran* comes from its base spirit, brandy.

The Kamiya Bar is located just outside the famous Asakusa shrine. For directions and hours, visit the website www.kamiya-bar.com.

## Midori Pine Soda

**1 oz (30 ml) Midori melon liqueur**
**4 oz (120 ml) pineapple juice**
**¹⁄₂ oz (15 ml) club soda**

Pour all ingredients into a highball glass over ice.

## MIDORI

Midori melon liqueur is made with Japan's famous superpremium green melon grown in Yubari. A top-grade Yubari melon can cost more than 10,000 yen.

Midori first came to the United States in 1978 with a monster launch event at Studio 54, attended by the stars of *Saturday Night Fever*, including a young John Travolta. The brand didn't hit the Japanese market until 1984. Today Midori is enjoyed in refreshing cocktails in more than thirty countries worldwide.

## Ginger Upper

6 fresh mint leaves

$1/4$ oz (7 ml)
    elderflower
    liqueur

$1\,1/2$ oz (45 ml) gin

3 oz (90 ml)
    grapefruit juice

Ginger ale

Fresh mint leaves
    for garnish

Muddle mint with
elderflower liqueur
in a mixing glass.
Pour gin and
grapefruit juice and
shake with ice.
    Pour into a
highball glass over
ice cubes. Top with
ginger ale, garnish
with mint leaves,
and serve.

## Ginger Beelu

3 parts Japanese
    beer

2 parts ginger ale

Yuzu salt for
    glass rim

Lemon wedge
    for garnish

Pour beer, then
ginger ale into a
yuzu salt–rimmed
glass.
    Garnish with
a lemon wedge
and serve.
    In Japan, "beer"
is pronounced
*bee-lu*.

more cocktails

## Fuji Apple Martini

**2 oz (60 ml) vodka**
**2 oz (60 ml) fresh**
 **Fuji apple juice**
**$\frac{1}{4}$ oz (7 ml)**
 **Triple Sec**
**$\frac{1}{2}$ tsp (2.5 ml)**
 **lemon juice**
**Apple wedge**
 **for garnish**

Mix all ingredients
except apple wedge
in a cocktail shaker
with ice.

Strain into a
chilled martini glass,
garnish with an
apple wedge,
and serve.

## Red Eye

**4 oz (120 ml)**
**Japanese beer**
**2 oz (60 ml)**
**tomato juice**
**1 tsp (5 ml)**
**lemon juice**
**Lemon wedge**
**for garnish**

Pour beer first,
then tomato juice
and lemon juice
into a highball
glass and stir.
 Garnish with
lemon wedge
and serve.

*m o r e   c o c k t a i l s*

## Kabosu Gimlet

2 oz (60 ml) gin
$^1/_2$ oz (15 ml)
   kabosu juice
$^1/_4$ oz (7 ml)
   gum syrup
Lime wheel for
   garnish

Mix all ingredients
except lime wheel
in a cocktail shaker
with ice.
   Strain into a
chilled martini glass,
garnish with a lime
wheel, and serve.

*more cocktails*

## Japanese-Brazilian

**4 slices Japanese
cucumber**
**¹/₂ oz (15 ml)
sugarcane juice**
**1 ¹/₂ oz (45 ml)
cachaça**
**¹/₂ oz (15 ml)
Kuromaru imo
jochu (sweet
potato shochu)**
**3 oz (90 ml)
pineapple juice**
**¹/₄ oz (7 ml)
lime juice**

Muddle cucumbers
with sugarcane
juice. Pour into a
cocktail shaker, add
cachaça, shochu,
pineapple juice, and
lime juice, and mix
with ice.

Pour into a tall
glass and serve.

## Brazilian Jiu Jitsu

2 whole strawberries, stemmed
   and rinsed
1/4 oz (7 ml) sugarcane juice
2 oz (60 ml) cachaça
1 oz (30 ml) crème de cassis
Club soda
Strawberry for garnish

Muddle strawberries with sugarcane juice in a mixing glass. Pour into a cocktail shaker, add cachaça and crème de cassis, and shake with ice.

Pour into a rocks glass. Top with club soda, garnish with a strawberry, and serve.

The number of people of Japanese decent living in Brazil is estimated at about 1.3 million, according to Japan's Ministry of Foreign Affairs. In 1918, the ship *Kosato-Maru* brought the first group of Japanese immigrants to Brazil. For nearly one hundred years, Brazil has had the largest population of Japanese people outside of Japan. A significant amount of trade has existed between Japan and Brazil, with Japan importing more goods than exporting into Brazil.

## Chinatown Rendezvous

1 ¹/₂ oz (45 ml)
    ginger-flavored
    vodka
1 tsp (5 ml)
    yuzu juice
1 tsp (5 ml)
    rosemary syrup
1 oz (30 ml) blood
    orange juice
Fresh rosemary
    sprig for garnish

Mix all ingredients
except rosemary
sprig in a cocktail
shaker with ice.
    Strain into a
chilled martini
glass, garnish with
rosemary sprig,
and serve.

## CHINATOWN

Yokohama Chinatown, or *Chukagai,* is the largest Chinatown in Japan. In 1859, when the port of Yokohama was first opened to foreign trade, Chinese traders began settling in the area. In Yokohama Chukagai, there are many stores and restaurants with colorful Chinese gates and buildings. For information on how to get to Chinatown, visit the Yokohama Chinatown website at www.chinatown.or.jp.

## Zen Kissaten

**1 $\frac{1}{2}$ oz (45 ml) Zen Green Tea Liqueur**
**3–4 oz (90–120 ml) steamed milk**
**Matcha powder for garnish**

Pour green tea liqueur and milk into a tea cup. Sprinkle with matcha powder and serve.

## JAPANESE CAFÉS

Kissaten refers to a Japanese café. Most *kissaten* shops serve coffee and tea as well as some soft drinks. Many also offer fresh pastries and desserts.

## Lady Godzilla

4–5 fresh mint
  leaves
$^1/_4$ oz (7 ml)
  umeshu
1 $^1/_2$ oz (45 ml)
  blanco tequila
1 oz (30 ml) Midori
  melon liqueur
$^1/_4$ oz (7 ml)
  lemon juice
Fresh mint sprig
  for garnish

Muddle mint leaves
with *umeshu* in a
mixing glass. Add
tequila, Midori, and
lemon juice and
shake with ice.

Strain into a
chilled martini glass,
garnish with mint
sprig, and serve.

## Melon Kakigori

2 oz (60 ml) Midori
  melon liqueur
1 scoop vanilla ice
  cream

Fill a martini glass
with shaved ice.
Pour Midori on top.
Top with a scoop of
vanilla ice cream.
Serve with a small
tea spoon.

You can substitute
Midori with Zen
Green Tea Liqueur.

### SHAVED ICE

*K*akigori is a
Japanese shaved-
ice dessert
flavored with
syrup.

more cocktails

## Melon Cream Soda

**1 oz (30 ml) Midori melon liqueur**
**1 1/2 oz (45 ml) citrus-flavored vodka**
**3 oz (90 ml) club soda**
**1 scoop vanilla ice cream**
**Melon slice for garnish**

Mix all liquid in a cocktail shaker with ice.
Pour into a tall glass. Top with vanilla ice
cream. Garnish with a melon slice.

   Melon cream soda, or melon soda, is
a green, nonalcholic drink that's a favorite
among children, often served at restaurants
or *kissaten* cafés.

## Shikoku Island Iced Tea

**4 lime chunks**
**Lemongrass**
**1 oz (30 ml)**
  **cachaça**
**2 oz (60 ml) saké**
**1/2 oz (15 ml)**
  **umeshu**
**Juice of 1/2**
  **mandarin**
  **orange**

Muddle lime and lemongrass in a mixing glass. Pour cachaça, saké, *umeshu*, and mandarin orange juice and shake with ice. Pour into a short glass and serve.

Shikoku Island is one of the four main islands of Japan and consists of four prefectures: Kochi, Ehime, Kagawa, and Tokushima. *Shikoku* literally means "four countries." To visit Shikoku Island, you can take either a ferry or plane from Honshu (main) Island. The Great Seto Bridge also connects Shikoku to Honshu Island. The Shikoku Railway Company or JR Shikoku also has several lines offering connections throughout the islands.

◀ The Great Seto Bridge

## Tokyo M&M

**2 oz (60 ml)**
  **Kentucky straight**
  **bourbon**
**2 oz (60 ml) chilled**
  **mugi cha**
  **(barley tea)**
**1/4 oz (7 ml)**
  **yuzu wine**
**Orange peel for**
  **garnish**

Pour all ingredients except orange peel into an old-fashioned glass over fresh ice. Stir, garnish with an orange peel, and serve.

# Ikebana

1 $\frac{1}{2}$ oz (45 ml)
   Kentucky Straight
   bourbon
1 $\frac{1}{2}$ oz (45 ml) grape
   juice
$\frac{1}{2}$ oz (15 ml)
   crème de cassis
$\frac{1}{2}$ tsp (2.5 ml)
   lemon juice
$\frac{1}{4}$ oz (7 ml)
   rose nectar
Edible rose petals
   for garnish
Fresh mint sprig
   for garnish

Mix all ingredients
except garnishes in
a cocktail shaker
with ice.
   Strain into a
chilled martini glass.
Garnish with edible
rose petals and a
mint sprig and serve.

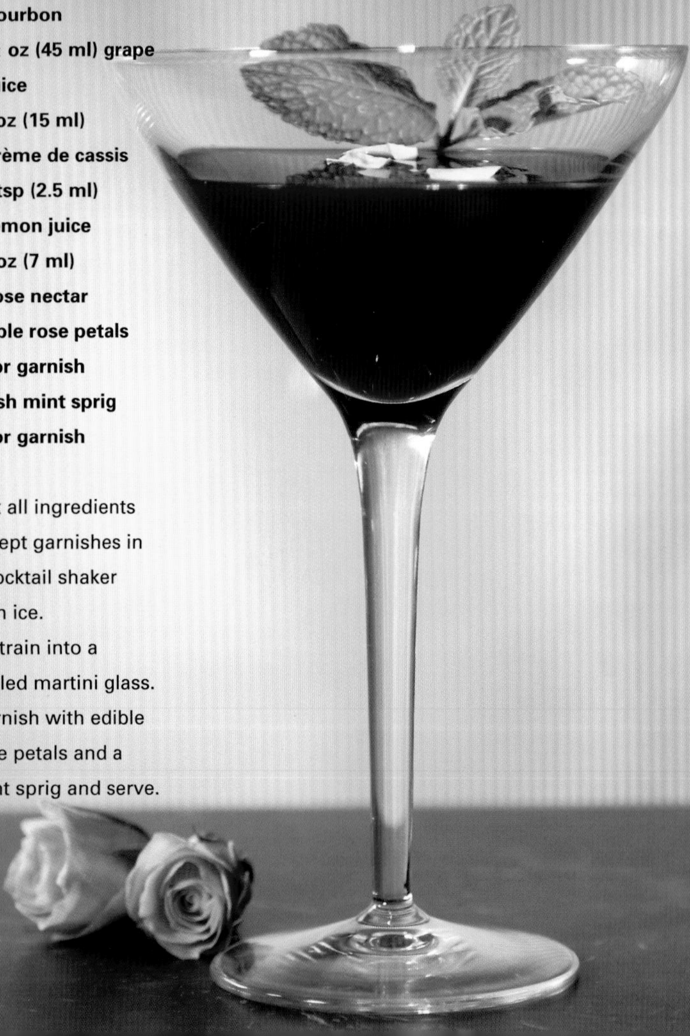

m
o
r
e

c
o
c
k
t
a
i
l
s

Traditionally, a
Japanese flower
arrangement is
called an *ikebana*.
It is carefully
constructed with
flowers, leaves,
and branches to
compose elegant
combinations of
natural figures
and colors.

## Yuzu Mojito

**6 fresh mint leaves**
**4 lime chunks**
**1 tsp (5 ml)**
    **gum syrup**
**2 oz (60 ml)**
    **light rum**
**1/4 oz (7 ml)**
    **yuzu juice**
**Club soda**

Muddle mint
leaves, lime,
and gum syrup.
    Pour into a cocktail
shaker, add rum
and yuzu juice,
and shake with ice.
    Pour into a
highball glass,
top with club soda,
stir, and serve.

## Yamanashi Sangria

**1 Fuji apple**
**1 nashi pear**
**Champagne grapes,**
    **skinned (or green**
    **grapes, sliced)**
**4 oz (120 ml)**
    **gum syrup**
**25 oz (750 ml)**
    **Chardonnay**

Cut fruits into chunks.
In a jar, add fruits,
gum syrup, and wine
and stir.
    Let mixture set
in the refrigerator for
at least 12 hours
before serving.

# ACKNOWLEDGMENTS

I raise my glass to all the people who contributed their time and effort in helping me write this book. I cannot *arigato* my family enough for putting up with me for all these years. Without them, this book could not have come to life. I'd also like to *domo arigato* the Japan National Tourism Organization (JNTO) for their resources. And, of course, there are so many others who made it possible for me to complete this book. If I have forgotten to credit anyone, my apologies, and please contact me; drinks are on me!

*Arigato* and *kanpai* to Suntory Ltd., SKYY Spirits LLC, Truth Be Told, Gekkeikan Sake Co. Ltd., The Jizake Inc., Stolzle USA, American Airlines, Pacific Institute for Research and Evaluations (PIRE), Toshimaya Sake Brewery, Hall PR, and Ozeki Sake.

Be sure to check out our updated blog about this book and more at www.cocktailtimes.com. If you'd like to receive spirited newsletters, you can sign up to become a VIP member at www.cocktailtimes.com/vip.

All photographs by Chris Roche, Snap Studio, except for photographs on pages 7, 8 (bottom left) by Gekkeikan Sake Company; 8 (right top and bottom), 9, 10 (top and bottom right), 11–15, 18–19, 26, 41, 48 (left), 55, 56–57 (left), 58 (right), 59, 60 (top left and right), 61 (top and bottom left), 68, 71, 75 by Yuri Kato; 30, 33, 38–39, 46, 52, 63, 73, 76 by Sakagucchan; 17 by Toshimaya Saké Brewery. Photographs on pages 28, 40, 50–51, 64, 85 (bottom left) © Getty Images. Photograph on page 88 © JNTO. Photograph on page 53 © Yasufumi Nishi/JNTO. Photographs on pages 1–6, 16, 20–25, 27, 29, 31–32, 34–37, 42–45, 47, 49, 54, 55 (right), 57 (right), 58 (left), 60 (bottom left), 61 (bottom left), 62, 65–67, 69–70, 72, 73 (left), 75 (left), 77–84, 85 (top right), 86–92 © Suntory Ltd.

# INDEX